To Mamma: It's thanks to you that I learned to love food

LOVE FOOD

AMORUSO'S
ITALIAN COOK BOOK

Photographs by ALAN PEEBLES
Edited by KAY COX
Design by LESLEY REDFERN

LOVE FOOD
Lorenzo Amoruso's Cook Book

Published by the Daily Record,
One Central Quay,
Glasgow, G3 8DA.

Edited and designed by First Press Publishing,
One Central Quay, Glasgow, G3 8DA.

ISBN 0-9544202-1-7

Printed and bound in Scotland

FIRST PRESS
PUBLISHING
DAILY RECORD AND SUNDAY MAIL MAGAZINE DIVISION

CONTENTS

FOREWORD

FOREWORD

LORENZO has been a regular at the restaurant since he came over here to play for Rangers, and we're always glad to see him.

He's like one of the family now, and though we may not cook exactly like his Mamma, Lorenzo is a man who enjoys his food - he knows what he likes and he knows he can get it from us, sitting in the regular booth that he likes in the corner.

Of course, as a professional athlete he looks after his body and generally eats the kind of thing that's good for him. There's one dish he enjoys above all others and he nearly always asks for it in advance - the marinaded grilled vegetables, which is why it's one of the recipes from the restaurant included in this book.

It's been a pleasure to have Lorenzo as a customer, and great fun to do the photo shoot here with him.

And he knows that when the time comes for him to give up football he can always get a job in our kitchen!

TONY CIMMINO & CLAUDIO NARDONI
Owners of O' Sole Mio Restaurant, Glasgow

9

INTROD

I DIDN'T learn to cook from a recipe book, or from a TV programme or school lessons. I learned to cook by phone – calling Mamma at home in Southern Italy at all hours to ask her what to do. I knew what I wanted to eat, maybe even had an idea what I needed to make it, but had no idea how to go about it. So I called Mamma to cry help... I still do sometimes.

When I was growing up in Bari, life was very straightforward – the woman stayed at home and did all the cooking, that's just the way it was. It's all changed now, of course. But back then, my sister Angelica would go in the kitchen with Ma and learn from her how to cook, boys didn't do any of that stuff. I was outside all the time, playing football, and I came in when I was hungry.

It was a nice way to grow up, I have to admit, always having the comfort of Ma there in a welcoming kitchen full of good food. But of course, when I needed to cook for myself, I had no idea what to do. I remember when I was 18 I was living away from home, working hard, getting back late... starving. I started with simple things – really simple, say scrambled eggs. Even then I might have to phone Ma to ask what to do!

I had to eat though, so I had to keep trying. I would try plain pasta, then maybe pasta with tomato sauce, then tomato sauce with something else in it. I would try something for the first time and maybe it was no good, so I would do it a little different next time, and it got better, and I would develop it. If it didn't get better, I didn't do it again!

Mamma wasn't always there to help, so I had to work some of it out for myself, but at least I knew from what she used to cook, what I was aiming for. I still love her cooking, of course, and some of the recipes in this book are the things she made for me as a boy and now cook myself today.

Lots of people may not bother to make a meal for one, but I enjoy it. Of course, it's much better for two. I do sometimes have friends from the team at my house and enjoy making them a dinner, but the best thing is to make a romantic meal for two.

It's not something I would do for a first date, the girl might not feel comfortable coming to my place when she doesn't know me so well, for one thing. But it's a little bit special. I haven't cooked for many girls, it means something if I do it.

A beautiful dinner is something any man

UCTION

or woman can do to create a bit of romance, make someone feel special, and that's why I have included my favourite things to make for the occasion. Love and food go together naturally.

In fact, you can tell a lot from the way a person eats. If I see someone has cake and puts on chocolate sauce, ice cream and vanilla sauce, you can see that they are not decisive types. They can't even tell what the flavour of the cake is.

But you can also tell from what a girl eats, and how she eats it, what she will be like in bed. Someone who eats a lot, for instance, isn't going to go to the bedroom and be great. I don't care what they say about women with a good appetite having a good sexual appetite, it's not my experience. If you go to bed with your stomach full and bloated, you are not going to perform so well.

Another clue is what they drink. Red wine drinkers are different from white. Red is a stronger, more robust flavour, and women who drink it will be more assertive in bed.

There are other ways to tell, things to notice. It's an intuitive thing. It's about the way she cuts her meat, the way she drinks from her glass, how she sits at the table, the whole picture...and 99 per cent of the time I am right.

The only exception I have experienced was one woman who ate like a princess. So delicate. Tiny mouthfuls, held her glass very lightly and took little sips. She was absolutely wild in bed! I'm not saying I didn't enjoy it, it was great, but I was so shocked, I didn't expect it at all.

So, when cooking a romantic meal, my rule is not to have anything too heavy. I don't drink often, but a glass of dry white fruity wine is lovely to start the evening – I love Gewurztraminer from Alsace.

Then oysters are a good thing to have ready when she arrives, if she likes them.

For a starter, my favourite is warm seafood salad. If it's followed by lobster served with linguine it is ideal. You can get these ingredients in the supermarkets here easily enough.

If you can get porcini mushrooms in season, they are delicious in a salad with rocket, sliced parmesan, olive oil and balsamic vinegar. You can use the dried ones but they are much, much tastier fresh. The best ingredients are best served simply – white truffle is exquisite, simply sliced and served with tagliatelle and a little bit of butter. I would sometimes do a fillet steak, cooked medium rare, too.

It's important to set the scene. Soft music

'You can tell from what a girl eats and how she eats it what she will be like in bed... it's an intuitive thing but 99 per cent of the time I'm right'

INTRODUCTION

and soft lighting are good for seduction – candles are much better than white lights and my favourites are vanilla scented ones from Crabtree & Evelyn. I love them – you get used to the scent during the course of a candlelit dinner, and you don't always smell it, but even when you come downstairs in the morning...there it is, delicious. I use a vanilla body lotion too. It's a strong scent, but I like being able to smell it all day – when you turn over in the night you can still smell it on the skin, it's gorgeous.

If I was cooking for a woman for the first time, I would choose lobster because I think it makes a good impression. It says a

'For a romantic meal, my rule is not to have anything too heavy... I would choose lobster, because I think it makes a good impression'

lot. When you start seeing someone you want everything to be perfect, you want to show the best of yourself and hide the worst!

The sea is so big, so full of things we don't know, it's kind of mysterious, and maybe that's a good effect on an important date.

Of course, I know seafood is also supposed to be an aphrodisiac but on an early date in the relationship, you shouldn't need any of that, all that desire should already be there, for sure.

I always like to serve the food on plain white plates, and try to make it look attractive – maybe sprinkle some paprika round the edge of the plate.

Presentation is really important, it shows you have taken a little extra care over the meal. I once went to a beautiful restaurant in Mauritius where Alain Ducas is the chef

and the food was so beautifully presented that it was a shame to eat it.

One of the most romantic places I have seen is a restaurant in Capri. They asked me if I wanted a table on the outside or in the middle. I didn't realise the significance and asked for the outside, and was so glad. It was on the edge of a garden, looking out over the sea. Ever since then I have this idea of the perfect place to have a romantic meal, it must be where you can sit outside, where the moon shines on water and you can see its reflection. Beautiful.

Maybe you can't manage to have all that for a meal in your own home, but you can still make it romantic.

I like music by Toni Braxton, Whitney Houston or even some Elton John to set the mood. Some flowers are nice – not a big floral display, but something small and interesting for the table.

You need to make things that don't keep

INTRODUCTION

you in the kitchen all the time. You want to be sitting beside your lover as long as possible, so it's better to plan a meal where some things can be prepared in advance.

Organisation is the key with cooking. You'll see me in Tesco, pushing my trolley round with my list, I will have planned what I want for the whole week. I'm very organised. I eat a lot of red meat, and of course, pasta, and I buy organic whenever I can.

'It's a great thing to catch your own dinner. In Bari, I love to dive and catch fish with a spear gun and in Scotland I go shooting deer and ducks'

In Bari, where I grew up, it's all about fish and seafood – it's a seaside town after all. I adore it but I must admit you have to take more care to cook it, one minute too much is a disaster. With something like steak, it's not so important to be so accurate.

When I'm in Bari I love to go out diving and catch fish with a spear gun. It's a great thing to catch your own dinner. In Scotland I go shooting, so I can do a decent venison stew, and roast the ducks that I shoot. I also take them to the training ground for the chef there to cook for us, and sometimes to my favourite restaurant, O' Sole Mio, in Glasgow. I eat there at least once a week – that's why I have also included some of my favourite recipes from there.

I love the way Claudio the chef does the ducks, and whenever I go there, they have my favourite grilled vegetables prepared for me. Claudio and his partner, Tony, always give me a great welcome, and I have my own little booth in the corner where I always sit in comfort.

Now that I am better in the kitchen, I can confidently cook for family, and I have done Christmas dinner for a few friends, too, which is a great treat.

Years ago, my brother and some friends came to stay with me and I decided to cook for us all. I enjoy it, it's no problem for me, but this was a big deal because I hadn't been cooking for long. I sent them out with a shopping list then got to work – we had decided on pasta al forno, it takes a lot of preparation.

You have to make the meatballs and do layers of sauce and pasta, put it in the oven and wait, wait, wait. It took longer than I thought and we were so hungry, but it was worth it. You feel so proud when you have done something well for the first time. Now, I wouldn't cook something that I hadn't already tried before for guests.

I prefer to make it only for myself at the start. I do sometimes use ready-prepared

INTRODUCTION

> **'In football, you spend a lot of time in hotels. You eat what's there, not always what you want. I love to be at home and cook things I want to eat'**

sauces, but it's much better to do it yourself if you can. It's the way Ma would always do it, so I am used to it that way.

When I was growing up, the women just spent all the day in the kitchen, everything was home cooked. In Italy, there are many occasions when we have friends round to drink a beer or some wine, there was always some little things to eat like foccacine, panzerotti, frittata.

Of course, it's all different now and you can buy these things in shops, just like we can here. If she is very busy Mamma might buy some of them sometime, but mostly she still makes them herself, so it's always great to go home for a celebration.

In Italy, we eat our meals in a different way to here in Britain. We have a starter then almost every time we have pasta then a second main course of meat or fish, called the "secondi".

Sunday is a good day for the whole family to come together after they have all been working different hours through the week, and we often make this big sauce for ragu, but the sauce can also be used for the first dish with pasta, then you can use it with little rolls with parsley, garlic and cheese.

It's good to make a meal for a lot of people in an easy way.

Mamma is proud of her boy for mastering cooking, but when she comes to stay with me, she is very strict, she does all the cooking or we go out to eat – she may be proud, but there's no way she is letting me in her kitchen...even if the kitchen is in my house!

You can eat just about anything in Glasgow now, there are so many different kinds of restaurants, but I usually stick with Italian. As well as O' Sole Mio, I like L'Ariosto and La Lanterna, too.

But for me, it's always best to be home, doing my own thing. In football, you spend a lot of time in hotels. You eat what's there, and it's not always what you want, so I love to be at home and cook the things I actually want to eat.

It's not always easy learning to cook, but it certainly isn't impossible – I believe everyone should do it!

LORENZO AMORUSO

INTRODUCTION

GALLEY GALLERY

GALLEY GALLERY

'I started learning to cook with simple things - really simple, say scrambled eggs. Even then I might call Ma to find out what to do!'

23

GALLEY GALLERY

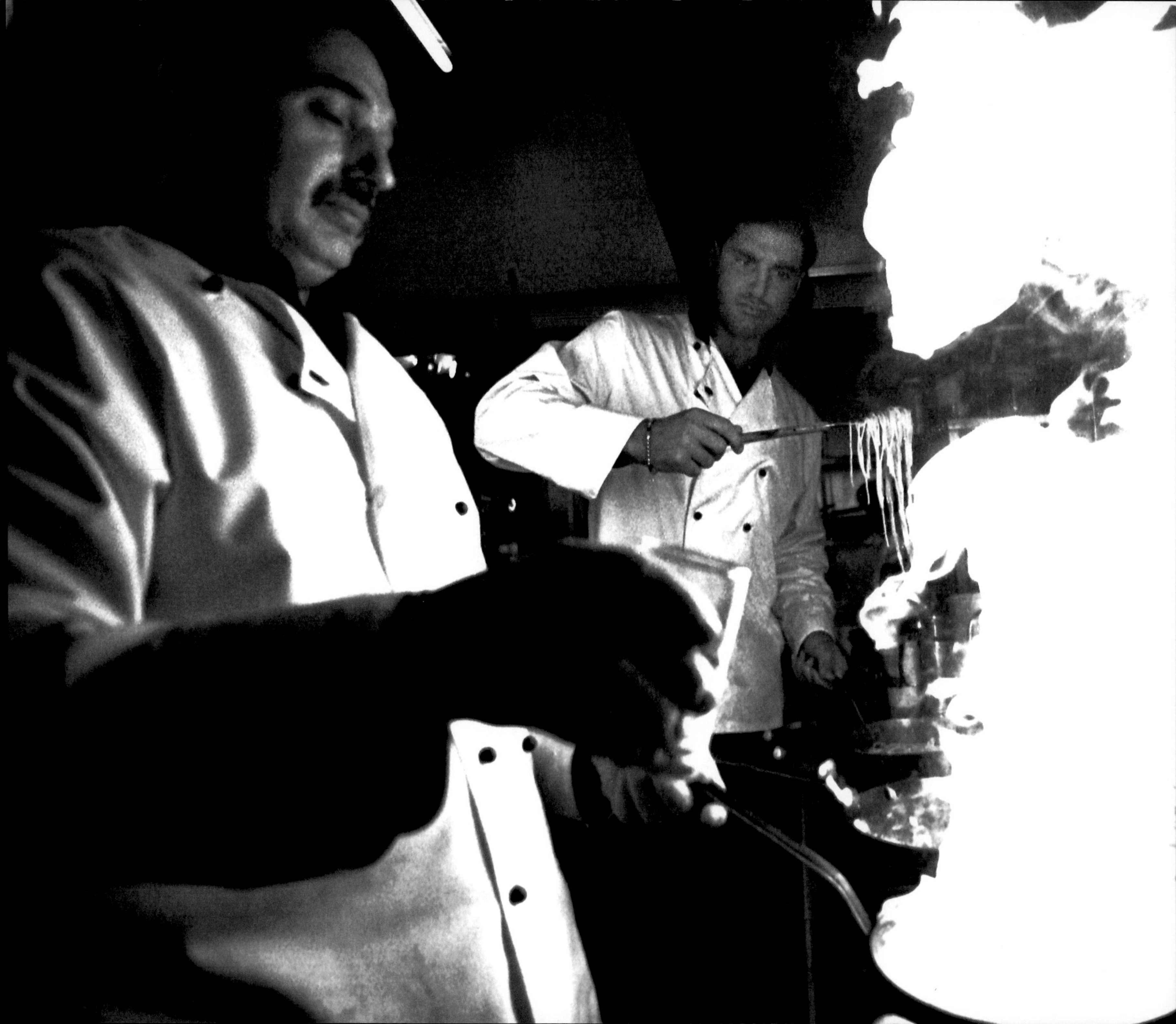

'I adore fish but I admit you have to take more care to cook it, one minute too much is a disaster. With steak, it's not so important.'

'Whenever I go to
O' Sole Mio, Claudio
has my favourite
grilled vegetables
prepared for me. Tony,
his partner, always
gives me a great
welcome. They say
when I am ready to
give up football I can
always get a job in the
kitchen...'

'Organisation is the key with cooking. You'll see me in Tesco, pushing my trolley round with my list. I will have planned what I want for the whole week. I eat a lot of red meat and, of course, pasta, and I buy organic when I can.'

GALLEY GALLERY

FOOD OF LOVE

SEAFOOD SALAD
Served Warm

Serves two

1 1 medium squid
2 500g/1lb mussels
3 150g/8oz raw prawns, shelled
4 125ml/3fl oz olive oil
5 2cloves garlic, cut into slivers
6 30ml/1fl oz White wine
7 squeeze of lemon juice
8 2tbsp Chopped parsley

'I like this much better warm than cold. You can buy any variation of shellfish, prepared if you prefer.'

To prepare

1 In a wide, shallow pan, add a dash of water and the raw mussles and steam until the shells open. Remove the mussels and discard the shells.

2 Clean the squid and cut it into rings. Set aside.

3 In the same pan, heat together the olive oil, wine and garlic. Simmer for about one minute

4 Add the prepared shellfish and turn the heat up to maximum and cook for about 2 minutes by which time the prawns should have changed to deep pink and the mixture is bubbling hot.

5 Add the lemon juice and parsley and serve while still sizzling hot.

PORCINI SALAD
On a Bed of Rocket Leaves

Serves two
1 115g/4oz small fresh porcini mushrooms, very thinly sliced
2 60g/2oz rocket leaves
3 2tblsp shavings of fresh parmesan cheese
4 extra virgin olive oil
5 mature balsamic vinegar
6 black pepper and sea salt

'It is essential to use fresh mushrooms for this, the dried ones just won't do.'

To prepare
1 Make a pile of rocket leaves on each plate.
2 Scatter the porcini over the leaves and douse with liberal amounts of olive oil and a drizzle of balsamic vinegar.
3 Grind over lots of black pepper and some sea salt.
4 Top with shards of parmesan.
5 Serve immediately.

OD OF LOVE

PORCINI & TRUFFLE
Served With Tagliatelle

Serves two
1 250g/8oz fresh tagliatelle
2 60g/2oz unsalted butter
3 250g/8oz porcini mushrooms, or closed cap mushrooms if you can't get porcini, sliced thinly
4 1 large egg yolk
5 4tsp white truffle oil

'Fresh porcini mushrooms are tastier than dried ones. They are delicious and are best when served simply.'

To prepare
1 Cook the pasta in a large amount of boiling salted water for 2-3 minutes.
2 In the meantime, melt the butter in a frying pan and add the mushrooms.
3 Cook over a medium heat until they are soft.
4 Transfer the mushrooms to a warm serving bowl, add the egg yolk and stir to break up.
5 Add the drained pasta, toss well and serve drizzled with the truffle oil.

LOBSTER
Served with Linguine

Serves two
1 250g/8oz linguine, fresh if possible
2 1tblsp olive oil
3 1tblsp butter
4 170g/6oz cooked lobster meat, sliced
5 1tblsp parsley chopped
6 1tbslp white wine
7 juice of a lemon
8 salt and freshly ground black pepper
9 slices of exotic fruit (papaya, mango or kiwi fruit) for garnish.

'I think lobster makes the right impression if you are cooking for a woman for the first time. It says a lot.'

To prepare
1 Cook the pasta al dente in a large amount of boiling salted water. Drain and set aside.
2 Heat the oil and butter in a large frying pan over a medium heat. Add the lobster meat and cook for 2-3 minutes.
3 Add the wine and lemon juice and season well.
4 Add the linguine and parsley and mix well over the heat for about 2-3 minutes.
5 Serve immediately topped with the sliced exotic fruits.

FOOD OF LOVE

GRILLED STEAK
With White Truffle

Serves two
1. 2 x 170g/6oz fillet steaks
2. olive oil
3. fresh truffle shavings
4. balsamic vinegar
5. salt and freshly ground black pepper.

'I eat a lot of red meat, and try to buy organic whenever I can.'

To prepare

1 Rub the steaks with olive oil and season with salt, pepper and vinegar. Grill under intense heat for five minutes each side for medium/pink meat.

2 Allow to rest for five minutes then add fresh truffle shavings.

3 This is great when served with sautéed spinach with garlic and chilli, and rosti potatoes. See Page 37 for details on how to cook these dishes.

FOOD OF LOVE

FO

ROSTI POTATOES
For the Grilled Steak

Serves two
1 small onion, finely chopped
2 olive oil
3 butter

4 250g/8oz waxy potatoes peeled,
salt and freshly ground black pepper

To prepare
1 Pre-heat the oven to 180ºC/375ºF/Gas Mark 4
2 Soften the onion in 1 tablespoon oil and remove from the heat.
3 Grate the potatoes coarsely, place in a bowl and season with salt. Leave to stand for 20 minutes, then squeeze dry.
4 Season with pepper and fork through the onion.
5 Heat 1tblsp butter with 1 tblsp oil in a frying pan.
6 Divide the potato mixture in two and drop each portion into the frying pan.
7 Pat the mixtures flat to make two little flat cakes.
8 Fry over a gentle heat until the underside is crusty and golden-brown (about 15 minutes). Shake the pan from time to time to prevent sticking.
9 Turn the rosti cakes over and cook for a further 5 minutes.
10 Now place the pan in a medium hot oven for about 10 minutes to ensure the potato is cooked through.

SAUTEED SPINACH
With Chilli

Serves two
1 250g/8oz fresh spinach, washed thoroughly and thick stems removed, salt

2 1 clove garlic cut into slivers
3 dash of hot chilli paste
4 1 tblsp extra-virgin olive oil

'I love spinach and the chilli finishes off the flavour just right.'

To prepare
1 Cook the spinach leaves in a covered pan with 1 tablespoon salt and with no more water than clings to them after being washed.
2 Cook until tender 5-10 minutes then drain well.
3 Put the garlic and olive oil in a large frying pan and cook until the garlic begins to colour. At this point lift it out and discard.
4 Now add the chilli and spinach to the hot oil. Toss over a high heat for a couple of minutes then serve.

OD OF LOVE

CREME BRULEE

Serves four
(It's very hard to make in quantities for two, so indulge yourself)

1 300ml/10 fl oz double cream
2 a vanilla pod, cut open and seeds discarded.

3 4-5 egg yolks
4 75g/3 oz caster sugar
icing sugar for glazing

To prepare

1 Place the double cream and vanilla in a thick-based pan and slowly bring to the boil. Whisk the egg yolks and sugar until white.
2 Add the cream to the sugar and slowly cook on a medium heat until the custard coats the back of a spoon.
3 Remove and quickly pour into individual dishes.

4 When cold and set sprinkle over the surface with icing sugar and glaze under a hot grill, allow to set again before serving but do not place in the fridge.

As a delicious alternative use a little less cream and once you have made the custard stir in a couple of tablespoons of Grand Marnier.

FOOD OF LOVE

BALSAMIC STRAWBERRIES
Serve Alone or with Almond Cake

Balsamic Strawberries
1 800g (2lbs) ripe strawberries, stemmed and halved
2 6tblsp balsamic vinegar
3 2tblsp honey
4 ½tsp freshly ground black pepper
5 1tblsp drained and rinsed green peppercorns, slightly crushed

To prepare
1 *In a bowl, gently combine all ingredients.*
Allow to stand, refrigerated, for at least 1 hour before serving.

Almond Cake
1 butter and flour for the cake tin
2 225g (8oz) marzipan
3 115g (4oz) unsalted butter, softened
4 170g (6oz) caster sugar
5 3 large eggs
6 grated lemon zest
7 2tblsp Grand Marnier or other orange brandy
8 35g (1oz) plain flour
9 ½tsp baking powder
10 icing sugar for dusting

To prepare
1 Preheat the oven to 180ºC/350ºF/GasMark 4. Lightly butter and flour a 20cm/8in round cake tin.
2 In the bowl of an electric mixer, combine the marzipan, butter, and sugar.
3 One at a time beat in the eggs, followed by the lemon zest and brandy.
4 Sift the flour and baking powder together.
5 Beat the flour into the marzipan-egg mixture until combined. Pour the batter in the prepared tin and bake for 35-40 minutes.
6 A skewer/toothpick inserted in the centre should come out clean. Cool on a rack before removing the cake from the tin.
7 Serve a wedge of the cake with a scoop of the balsamic strawberries. Dust with a sprinkling of icing sugar and place a dollop of the Orange Mascarpone on the cake.

Orange Mascarpone
1 250g(8oz) mascarpone cheese
2 grated zest and juice from an orange
3 1tblsp Grand Marnier or other orange liqueur

To prepare
1 In a bowl, combine all the ingredients, adding sufficient orange juice to achieve a dropping consistency and beat well. Let stand refrigerated, at least one hour before serving.

STARTERS

STARTERS

GRILLED VEGETABLES

Serves four

1	1 lemon	**6**	4 tsp olive oil
2	2 medium courgettes	**7**	2 cloves of garlic
3	2 mixed peppers (red & green)	**8**	salt and pepper
4	1 large aubergine	**9**	a pinch of oregano
5	1lb fresh mushrooms	**10**	flat parsley

'This is one dish I enjoy above all others. I always ask for it when I visit O' Sole Mio'

To prepare

1 Thickly slice vegetables.

2 Add salt, pepper, olive oil and chopped garlic Grill in a charcoal grill for approximately five minutes each side. (An ordinary grill can be used for this dish if you do not have a charcoal grill).

3 Serve with a touch of salt and pepper and chopped garlic. Add a sprinkle of parsley and the juice of a full lemon.

STUFFED PEPPERS

Serves four

1 4 large peppers
2 300g/10oz lean veal, finely minced
3 100g/3oz grated fresh parmesan cheese
4 2 eggs
5 1 medium buffalo mozzarella, grated
6 1tsp salt

7 2tblsp olive oil
8 2 cloves garlic
9 125g/4oz cherry tomatoes, roughly chopped
10 2tblsp parsley, chopped

'My favourite! I love peppers, I can even eat them in the morning, no problem. Every time I go home, Mamma will make this.'

To prepare

1 Pre-heat the oven to180ºC/375ºF/Gas Mark 4
2 Cut the top off the peppers and scoop out inside.
3 Beat the eggs, add the meat with salt and mozzarella and parmesan, mix together.
4 Stuff peppers with meat mixture and replace tops.

5 Place the oil, tomatoes, parsley, garlic, salt and some water in an ovenproof casserole just big enough to take the peppers in one layer.
6 Bring to the boil then carefully add the peppers, standing next to each other without touching.
7 Cover and place in the pre-heated oven for one hour or until cooked through.

STARTERS

STARTERS

MINI PANCETTA

& Asparagus Frittata

Makes twelve

1 1 large onion, finely diced
2 olive oil for frying
3 100g/3oz diced pancetta
4 200g/7oz asparagus, trimmed
5 7 large eggs
6 350ml/12fl oz double cream
7 85g/3oz parmesan cheese
8 salt and freshly ground black pepper

PARSLEY PANCETTA

& Red Onion Frittata

Serves four

1 1tblsp vegetable oil
2 55g/2oz frozen peas, defrosted, or fresh peas blanched until al dente
3 60g/2oz pancetta, diced
4 1 med potato, peeled
5 1 med red onion, peeled and sliced
6 1 clove garlic, peeled and finely chopped
7 5 eggs
8 55g/2oz butter
9 2 heaped tbsp chopped fresh parsley
10 60g/2oz grated gruyere cheese
11 sea salt and freshly ground black pepper

'We do frittata very often in Italy. After a good pasta, maybe you don't want a second course so you have a slice of this and it doesn't make you very full. You can have a thousand kinds, believe me - asparagus, cheese, potato, spinach, mushroom'

To prepare

1 Preheat the oven to 180°C/350°F/Gas Mark 4.
2 Lightly oil a 12-bun nonstick muffin tin.
3 Cut the asparagus diagonally into small pieces, keeping the tips whole. Cook until al dente in boiling salted water, drain and refresh.
4 Fry the onion in some oil until soft, add the pancetta to the pan.
5 Continue to fry until the pancetta is crisp.
6 Stir the asparagus into the onion mixture, season and divide between the muffin tins.
7 Using a fork, roughly mix together the eggs, cream, Parmesan and seasoning.
8 Pour into the muffin tins; bake in the centre of the oven for 20 minutes or until puffy but firm.

To prepare

1 Fry the diced pancetta in a frying pan over a medium heat in the oil until crisp, lift out and put in the sliced red onion and cook for 15 minutes or so over a medium to low heat, until softened and starting to brown at the edges.
2 Add the garlic and cook for one minute more. Remove with a slotted spoon, draining as much oil.
3 Boil the whole potato until just soft and dice into small pieces.
4 Meanwhile, preheat the grill.
5 In a large bowl whisk the eggs together, then put the pancetta, peas, potatoes, parsley, red onion and cheese into the bowl and mix thoroughly, then season with salt and a little pepper.
6 Heat a non-stick pan over a medium heat.
7 Add the butter and when it is foaming stir in the egg mixture.
8 Turn the heat down and cook gently until the base is set and only the centre is runny.
9 Slide the pan under the hot grill and cook for 2-4 minutes, until the frittata has set.
10 Remove the pan from the grill and serve as soon as possible.

FISH SOUP

Serves six-eight

1 1 large onion, chopped
2 2-3 cloves garlic
3 3-4tblsp olive oil
4 2 x 400g/14oz cans peeled plum tomatoes
5 1 large potato, peeled & diced
6 a handful of herbs including rosemary, thyme, basil and oregano

7 black pepper
8 a large glass of white wine
9 1tblsp white wine vinegar
10 2k/4½lb mixed fish-try to use warm water fish like red mullet, snapper, bream, gurnard for a more authentic soup plus some squid, mussels, langoustine or lobster.

'I don't eat a lot of soups, but if you are going to have soup, this is the one'

For garnish

1 Flat-leaf parsley, chopped

To prepare

1 Ask the fishmonger to clean and descale the fish and cut it into big chunks and to clean the squid and cut it into rings.
2 Wash and de-beard the mussels.
3 In a large saucepan, fry the onion and garlic in olive oil until golden.
4 Add the tomatoes, potato, herbs, black pepper, wine and vinegar.
5 Bring to the boil and turn down the heat and simmer for 15 minutes.

6 Now add the fish in order of cooking times:
7 Live Lobster allow 4 minutes per lb (cooked lobster-just reheat)
8 Chunks of fish no more than 5 minutes in total
9 Langoustine and Mussels allow 2 minutes in total.
10 Serve the fish in it's broth sprinkled with the chopped parsley, from a large terrine with chunks of bread.

50

ASPARAGUS
with Crispy Pancetta &
Black Olive-Caper Dressing

Serves four
1 500g/1lb asparagus, trimmed and left whole

For the vinaigrette:
1 2 shallots, finely chopped
2 1tblsp olive oil
3 1tblsp capers, chopped
4 1tblsp black olives, pitted and

2 salt and freshly ground black pepper
3 fresh basil leaves

chopped
5 75g/3oz thinly sliced pancetta
6 2tblsp balsamic vinegar
7 50ml/2fl oz extra virgin olive oil

'This is good for a starter, and it looks nice on the plate, too, if you can do it properly.'

To prepare
1 Cook the asparagus in boiling salted water for two minutes, drain and cool under running cold water.
2 Drain and sprinkle with salt. Set aside.
3 To make the vinaigrette, brown the shallots in oil. Reduce the heat and add the capers and olives. Remove from the heat and add the oil and vinegar. Set aside.

4 Grill the pancetta until crispy, and crumble into small pieces.

5 To serve, toss the asparagus in a frying pan with oil over a high heat, serve on warm plates, drizzled with the vinaigrette. Sprinkle over the crispy pancetta and garnish with sprigs of basil.

STARTERS

STARTERS

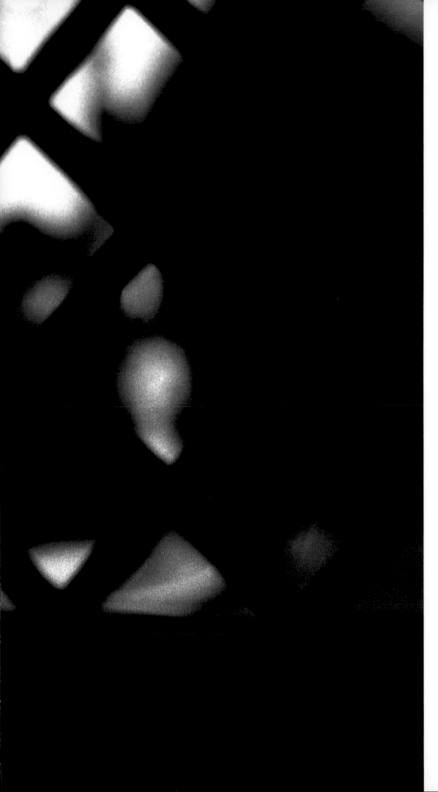

STUFFED MUSSELS

Serves four

1 20 large uncooked mussels
2 10 slices bread made into breadcrumbs
3 6 eggs
4 100g/3½oz grated fresh parmesan cheese
5 2tsp salt
6 4tblsp parsley

7 4tblsp vegetable oil
8 1k/2lb peeled plum tomatoes,
  chopped (4 tins)
9 olive oil
10 garlic

'Another dish from Bari, this one reminds me of my childhood. You can also use the sauce for pasta.'

To prepare

1   Beat eggs, add salt, parsley and cheese. Mix in sufficient breadcrumbs to make a paste.
2   Wash mussels, open slightly with a sharp knife and stuff with paste.
3   Fry mussels in vegetable oil until the paste is golden.

4   Put the olive oil and garlic into a large casserole pot and soften over a gentle heat.
5   Add the tomatoes and 150ml/5fl oz water and cook for 10 mins.
6   Add mussels and simmer uncovered slowly for 30 mins.

SNACKS

SNACKS

BRUSCHETTA
with White Bean Puree & Parma Ham

I remember when I was young there was a period where there were good tomatoes, but now you can get them all the year round. Probably every restaurant in italy has got a version of this, and anybody can make it. it's nice to offer people when they come to your house, the red colour of the tomatoes is attractive

Serves four

1 75ml/3fl oz olive oil plus extra for drizzling
2 3 cloves garlic, crushed
3 2 tsp finely chopped rosemary leaves
4 1 tin cannellini beans

5 squeeze of lemon juice
6 salt & freshly ground black pepper
7 125g/4 oz parma ham
8 4 slices country bread

'Probably the most famous Italian snack. You can do it just with tomatoes, but it's something you can change, you can add tuna, or pieces of onion, anything.'

To prepare

1 Drain the cannellini beans and reserve the liquid.
2 Combine the olive oil, garlic and rosemary and cook over a gentle heat until the garlic is soft, but without colouring.
3 Add the beans, stir to combine and cook covered for about 10 mins.
4 Moisten with a little of their liquid if necessary. Mash or pulse in a food processor to make a coarse puree.
5 Season to taste with lemon juice, salt and pepper.
6 Toast the bread on both sides, drizzle with olive oil and top with bean puree and garnish with slices of Parma ham.
7 Serve with tossed salad leaves.

FOCCACINE

Serves four
1. 1kg/2lb strong flour
2. 1 sachet easy-blend dried yeast
3. 500g/1lb potatoes
4. 4tblsp olive oil
5. 1tsp salt
6. 170g/6oz cherry tomatoes, chopped
7. 2tsp dried oregano

'In Italy we celebrate your saint's name, it's not a party like a birthday, people will say congratulations and come to your house to drink a beer or wine. You can make little things to eat, some salty some sweet.'

To prepare
1. Peel potatoes, cut into chunks and boil. When soft, mash and leave to cool.
2. Mix flour with yeast and oil, salt add potato and sufficient warm water to form a pliable dough.
3. Roll into walnut sized balls. Place, well-spaced in the bottom of an ovenproof gratin dish or something similar.
4. Leave in a warm place and allow to rise for 60 minutes.
5. Pre-heat oven to 180ºC/375ºF/Gas Mark 4.
6. Add tomato, sprinkle with salt and oregano and cook for 20 minutes or until golden brown.

SNACKS

RICOTTA TORTA
With Herbs

This is another thing that we do especially in the South of Italy. There was a period when there was not enough food and people couldn't have meat, but they made cheese. It's very fresh and very good.

Serves six

1 1k/2lb ricotta
2 3 eggs, separated
3 3tblsp chopped flat-leaf parsley
4 3tblsp chopped basil
5 1tsp finely chopped rosemary
6 1tsp finely chopped thyme
7 1tsp finely chopped sage
8 3tblsp freshly grated pecorino romano cheese
9 salt and freshly ground black pepper to taste
10 25g/1oz butter
11 2tblsp breadcrumbs

'Not generally used as a dinner. You can use this if there is a party at your house. Two slices will make you full.'

To prepare

1 Drain the ricotta and place in a mixing bowl and, using a wooden spoon, stir in the egg yolks.
2 Add the herbs, grated pecorino romano cheese and salt and pepper to taste. Beat the egg whites until stiff and gently fold into the mixture.
3 Preheat the oven to 200°C/400°F Gas Mark 6.
4 Generously butter a round, high-sided cake tin or a 22cm/10ins springform tin and sprinkle with breadcrumbs.
5 Pour in the ricotta mixture.
6 Bake the ricotta torta in the oven for 1 hour, or until the top of the torta is firm to the touch and golden.
7 Remove from the oven and let rest for about 5 minutes. As it cools, it will shrink. Unmould the torta and cut into wedges, serve with mixed salad leaves.

CHEESE TARTS
With Cherry Tomatoes

Makes four

1 25g/1oz butter
2 20cm/9ins square of ready-rolled chilled puff pastry
3 1 large egg
4 1 generous tblsp ricotta or mascarpone
5 25g/1oz gruyere cheese, grated
6 1tsp Dijon mustard
7 several sprigs of fresh herbs, or several pinches of dried herbs
8 2 fresh ripe tomatoes, blanched and skinned
9 225g/8oz canned chopped tomatoes, well drained
10 15g/½oz freshly grated Parmesan cheese
11 salt and freshly ground black pepper
12 flour, for dusting

To prepare

1 Preheat the oven to 220°C/425°F/Gas Mark 7.
2 Cut 4 x 4 inch circles from the puff pastry and place on a non-stick baking sheet. Re-roll the remaining pastry and cut it into 1 cm strips. Dampen the edges of the pastry circles with water and lay the prepared strips around the edges to form a border. Slit the border with a knife at regular intervals. In a bowl, lightly whisk the egg. Remove 1tblsp of it and put this in a saucer. Add a few drops of water to the saucer and brush this egg and water mixture lightly over the pastry rim. Return any remaining egg and water to the bowl.
3 Whisk in the ricotta or mascarpone, the grated gruyere, the mustard and herbs. Season generously.
4 Thinly slice the fresh tomatoes, discarding the seeds and excess pulp.
5 Stir the drained canned tomatoes into the seasoned egg and cheese mixture. Spoon the mixture over the pastry, spreading it evenly.
6 Arrange the tomato slices on top.
7 Sprinkle with the parmesan and a little extra pepper. Dot with butter.
8 Bake for 20-30 minutes, until golden and cooked through. Check after 15-20 minutes: if the topping is browning too fast, cover loosely with lightly crushed foil.
9 With a spatula check that the pastry base is crisp enough before removing from the oven.
10 Serve warm rather than piping hot.

SNACKS

PANZEROTTI

Serves six
1 1kg/2lb flour
2 1 sachet of easy blend yeast
3 500g/1lb mozzarella
4 100ml/4fl oz olive oil
5 500g/1lb grated Parmesan cheese
6 1 tsp salt
7 vegetable oil for frying

'Kind of like a closed pizza. Fry lots of them – great for groups of people watching the game on TV.'

To prepare
1 Melt yeast in hot water and mix with flour, olive oil and teaspoon of salt.
2 Put dough in container and close. Leave to rise for 60 minutes.
3 Cut the dough into pieces and make into small pizzas.
4 Put spoonful of mozzarella and Parmesan into centre of pizza and fold like an envelope.
5 Shallow Fry.

PIZZA DE PATATE

1 1 kg potatoes
2 4 eggs
3 100g cooked ham
4 100g grated parmesan
5 300g mozzarella
6 4 tblsp breadcrumbs
7 4 tblsp olive oil plus extra for drizzling
8 Salt
9 150ml/5floz milk

To prepare
1 Peel potatoes, boil until soft and mash.
2 Pre-heat oven to 180ºC/375ºF/Gas Mark 4
3 Cut ham and mozzarella into small piecesand stir through the mashed potatoes.
4 Beat eggs in a large bowl with a pinch of salt and the milk. Add the potato mixture and beat together.
5 Heat the olive oil in a large frying pan and pour in the potato/egg mixture.
6 Press down.
7 Sprinkle with breadcrumbs. Drizzle olive oil on top.
8 Bake in oven for 20 mins. Serve in wedges.

CKS

PARMIGLIANI
Di Melanzani

Serves four

1 1kg/2lb aubergines
2 5 eggs
3 300g/10oz mozzarella, grated
4 100g/3oz fontina cheese, grated
5 100g/3oz cooked ham, chopped
6 1k/2lb peeled plum tomatoes, chopped
7 2 tblsp olive oil
8 2tsp salt
9 flour
10 vegetable oil for shallow frying
11 1 onion

'Another that you can use as a starter or for a snack. Delicious.'

To prepare

1 Pre-heat the oven to180ºC/375ºF Gas Mark 4
2 Peel aubergines and slice. Dust in flour.
3 Beat eggs, add salt and 50g fontina cheese.
3 Dip slices of aubergines into egg mixture to coat and fry in vegetable oil.
4 In a large saucepan, fry the onions in the olive oil until golden.
5 Add the tomatoes, 150ml/5fl oz of water and salt.
6 Simmer for 15 minutes until thickened to a sauce.
7 Pour some sauce into an ovenproof baking dish.
8 Make a layer of aubergines, scatter over some chopped ham and grated mozzarella and fontina. Pour over some more tomato sauce and repeat the layers finishing with some tomato sauce.
9 Cook for 30 minutes in the pre-heated oven

PIZZA MARGHERITA

Serves one/two

1 500g/1lb flour
2 1½tsp easy-blend yeast
3 1tsp salt
4 1tblsp olive oil plus extra for drizzling
5 200ml/7floz water

6 100ml/4floz milk
7 salt and freshly ground blackpepper
8 1 buffalo mozzarella, sliced
9 250g/8oz peeled chopped tomatoes
10 50g/2oz grated Parmesan

'I like my pizza simple and classic, I don't like lots of ingredients.'

To prepare

1 Mix together the flour, salt and yeast.
2 Warm together 200ml/7fl oz water and 100ml/4fl oz milk and stir into the flour with the olive oil.
3 Knead for 10 mins.
4 Leave in a large bowl, in a warm place, covered with a damp tea towel for 60 mins to rise.

5 Pre-heat the oven to 180ºC/375ºF Gas Mark 4
6 Roll into flat pizza pan oiled with a little olive oil.
7 Top with peeled chopped tomatoes, mozzarella, salt, pepper, Parmesan cheese and a drizzle of olive oil.
8 Cook for 30 mins.

SNACKS

PASTA
pasta

BASIC TOMATO
Sauce for Pasta

Serves four

1 1x400g/14oz tin peeled plum tomatoes
2 1 small onion, peeled and very finely chopped
3 2tblsp virgin olive oil
4 1 small clove garlic, peeled and crushed
5 1 small dried chilli, crumbled
6 salt and freshly ground black pepper
7 400g/14oz good-quality dried egg pasta
8 60g/2½ oz unsalted butter
9 4-rounded tblsp freshly grated Parmesan
10 1x15g/½oz pack fresh basil leaves, torn

'Easy, but at the same time healthy. Even when you come home hungry, it's just 10 minutes to make this.'

To prepare

1 Lift the tomatoes out of the tin, split them open and squeeze out and discard the watery liquid in the middle of each. Place in a food processor, along with the juices from the tin, and blend to a puree

2 In a medium pan, soften the onion in the oil over a medium heat for about 10 minutes, until soft. Add a little water as the onions cook to prevent browning.

3 Meanwhile, fill a large pan with water, and 2 rounded tsp of salt and put on to boil for the pasta. When the water is boiling, add the pasta and cook according to the instructions on the pack.

4 When the onion is soft, add the garlic, chilli, and tomato, and then bring to the boil and cook over a lively heat for no more then 3 minutes.

5 Taste and adjust the seasoning, then remove from the heat.

6 When the pasta is cooked, melt the butter in a large sauté pan, then slide in the drained pasta, give a stir and mix in the sauce and cheese. Stir-fry for no longer than a minute, then scatter with the basil and serve.

PASTA

PASTA
with Chickpeas

Very Mediterranean food, for sure. Some people eat chick peas without pasta, even. just cook them and eat them, maybe add olive oil, pepper, that's it. They are good, what our bodies need. This is a cross between a soup and a stew. Some good olive oil and chilli added at the end gives real attitude.

Serves four-six
1 225g/8oz chick peas   **2** 225g/8oz small shell pasta

For the stock
1 450g/1lb chicken wings   **4** 1 carrot
2 1 large onion   **5** 1 clove garlic
3 1 stick celery   **6** 3 bay leaves
                              7 salt

For the sauce
1 3-4 tbsp olive oil   **2** chilli sauce

To prepare
1 Soak the chick peas in water for a few hours or overnight.
2 Put the chicken wings in a large saucepan of cold water and bring to the boil.
3 Carefully skim the surface, add the vegetables, garlic, bay leaves and drained chick peas.
4 Simmer gently for at least an hour, covered.
5 When the chickpeas are tender, remove the chicken and bay leaves and season with salt. There should be plenty of liquid.
6 Add the pasta and cook for 12 minutes, stirring occasionally, adding water if necessary to prevent drying out.
7 Take 3 or 4 tablespoons of the hot stock add the same amount of olive oil and some chilli sauce, mix and pour it over the pasta.

SPAGHETTI
with Rich Lamb Ragu

Serves six

1 4tblsp olive oil
2 1½k(3lb) minced lamb
3 salt and freshly ground black pepper
4 1 large onion, sliced
5 3 cloves garlic, crushed
6 1 carrot, finely chopped
7 1 fennel bulb or 3 sticks celery, finely chopped
8 500g(1lb) tomatoes, peeled, deseeded, and chopped
9 100ml(4fl oz) red wine vinegar
10 60g(2oz) golden raisins
11 1 tblsp soft light brown sugar
12 200ml(7fl oz) chicken stock
13 100ml(4fl oz) red wine
14 1tblsp rosemary, chopped
15 1tsp cinnamon
16 500g(1lb) spagetti
17 2 tblsp parsley, chopped

To prepare

1 Heat 3tblsp of the olive oil in a heavy-bottomed casserole and brown the lamb. Remove the meat and set aside.
2 Add the onions, garlic, carrots, and fennel to the pan and sauté over a moderate heat until just beginning to colour.
3 Return the meat to the casserole and add the tomatoes, vinegar, raisins, sugar, stock, wine, rosemary, and cinnamon.
4 Season with salt and freshly ground black pepper.
5 Bring to the boil, then simmer gently with the lid on for 1 to 1½ hours, or until the meat is tender and the sauce thickened. Adjust the seasoning and keep warm.
6 To serve: Cook the pasta in salted boiling water until just al dente. Drain; toss with the remaining 1tblsp olive oil and the parsley. Ladle the lamb sauce over the pasta and garnish with toasted pine nuts.

FUSILLI
with Red Pesto Sauce

Serves six

1 400g/14 oz fusilli
2 olive oil for tossing the fusilli
3 150ml/5fl oz creme fraiche
4 1x400g/12fl oz tin chopped tomatoes
5 3 level tbsp red pesto sauce
6 salt and freshly ground pepper
7 fresh basil leaves and stoned black olives

'Great, fresh sauce. It has quite a light flavour and you can really enjoy it, I think. Quick and easy to make.'

To prepare

1 Combine the creme fraiche, the tin of tomatoes and the red pesto sauce, and simmer over a gentle heat for 20 mins until thick.
2 Cook the pasta until al dente in plenty of boiling salted water.
3 Strain, add the the red pesto sauce. Mix well, stir in the olives and roughly chopped basil leaves and serve immediately.

PASTA

PASTA AL FORNO

Serves four

1 500g/1lb dried rigatoni pasta
2 50g/2oz grated fresh
Parmesan cheese
3 250g/8oz lean veal, minced (use

beef if you prefer)
4 2 tsp salt
5 2 eggs
6 vegetable oil for shallow frying

For the sauce:

1 1 medium onion, chopped
2 1k/2lb peeled tomatoes, chopped
3 handful of basil shredded
4 4tblsp olive oil

5 500g/1lb mozzarella, grated
6 200g/7oz cooked ham, finely diced
7 fresh grated parmesan cheese

'Takes a long time to prepare but it's not difficult. You can make more and put some in the freezer.'

To prepare

1 Pre-heat the oven to
180ºC/375ºF/Gas Mark 4
2 Beat eggs with veal, add salt,
parmesan and form into meatballs.
3 Gently fry meatballs in vegetable oil,
on all sides until golden. Drain and set
aside.
4 In a large saucepan , fry the onions
in olive oil until golden.
5 Add 150ml/5fl oz of water, the

tomatoes and basil and cook for 15mins.
6 Cook pasta (al dente), drain and stir
in some tomato sauce.
7 Mix in the chopped ham, mozzarella
and meatballs,and add the rest of the
sauce.
8 Turn into an ovenproof dish and
sprinkle over the parmesan.
9 Cook for 30-40 mins in the
pre-heated oven.

PASTA

PENNE CHICKEN
& Spinach

Serves four

1. 1 packet of penne pasta (500g)
2. 2 chicken supreme, diced
3. 400g fresh spinach
4. 1 clove of garlic
5. 1 onion diced
6. olive oil
7. salt and pepper

'Another great favourite of mine... and its so easy to make.'

To prepare

1. Put olive oil in a large pan
2. Add diced garlic, onions & chicken
3. Blanche for around 10 minutes
4. When golden brown add spinach and cooked penne. Blanche together with a sprinkle of parmesan cheese, salt and pepper.
5. Finally, add a sprinkle of flat parsley

GNOCCHI
with Four Cheese Sauce

Serves four
1 500g/1pt milk
2 125g/4oz semolina
3 60g/2oz butter, plus extra
for greasing
4 1 large egg, beaten

5 90g/3oz parmesan cheese or gabriel,
freshly grated
6 salt and freshly ground black pepper
7 freshly ground nutmeg

To prepare
1 Bring the milk to the boil in a medium sized saucepan. Turn down the heat and stirring all the time, add the semolina in a steady stream.
2 Simmer gently for 2 minutes until the mixture is very thick and leaves the side of the pan.
3 Remove from the heat and stir in 25g/1oz of the butter, the egg and 50g/2oz

of the parmesan or gabriel cheese.
4 Stir well until the butter and cheese melt.
5 Season with ½ tsp salt and a good grinding of black pepper and nutmeg. Turn into a well-greased baking tin or pie dish to make a layer about 1½cm/ ½ inch thick. Allow to cool and set for at least two hours or overnight.

Cheese Sauce
1 1oz butter
2 450ml/1pt full-cream milk
3 2 egg yolks
4 2oz gorgonzola, crumbled

5 5oz emmantal, grated
6 5oz mascarpone
7 30g/1oz parmesan cheese, finely grated

To prepare
1 Melt the butter in a small saucepan. Pour on a little of the milk. Add the cheeses, stir together, heating gently until melted, adding more milk, if required, to give the sauce a homogeneous, creamy consistency. Remove from the heat. Whisk in the egg yolks.
2 Preheated oven Gas Mark 6 200°C/400°F
3 Turn out the semolina mixture on to

a work surface and cut into squares, bars or circles using a small pastry cutter.
4 Place in a single layer in the dish, pour over the cheese sauce and season with black pepper.
5 Cook in the pre-heated oven for 30-35 minutes until the cheese is bubbling and golden brown. If necessary, finish browning under a hot grill.

PA

SPAGHETTI
Alla pescatora

Serves four

1 500g/1lb cooked mixed seafood (mussels, prawns, shrimp, squid etc)
2 2 cloves garlic, crushed
3 4 tblsp olive oil
4 10 cherry tomatoes, chopped
5 300g/10 oz spaghetti
6 salt and freshly ground blackpepper
7 2 tblsp chopped parsley

'You can use whatever fish you want in the pasta. Don't add the tomatoes if you prefer a stronger taste of the sea.'

To prepare

1 In a large saucepan soften the garlic in the olive oil without browning.
2 Add the tomatoes plus 150ml/5fl oz of water and simmer over a low heat for 5 mins.
3 Add mixed cooked fish and the parsley and heat through. Season to taste.
4 Cook spaghetti al dente. Drain and return to pan.
5 Leave on stove and stir in the fish mixture. Serve right away.

PORCINI LASAGNE

Serves six

1 500g/1lb Lasagne sheets

For the filling

2 150g/5oz butter
3 60g/2oz flour
4 1.2 litres/40fl oz milk
5 200g/7oz flat-capped mushrooms
6 25g/1oz porcini, dried (ceps)
7 60ml/3fl oz extra virgin olive oil
8 200g/7oz Parma ham, cut into
julienne strips
9 200ml/7fl oz single cream
10 3 tblsp parsley, finely chopped
11 150g/5oz parmesan cheese, freshly grated
12 truffle oil
13 salt and freshly ground black pepper

'Good... fantastic, actually. People like lasagne because it has everything, poricini, cheese, meat, sauce.'

To prepare

1 Soak the dried porcini in water overnight.
2 To make the sauce, melt 60g/2oz butter, add the flour and blend in well.
3 Heat the milk and add a little at a time, beating well with a balloon whisk. Bring to a simmer.
4 Cook the flat-capped mushrooms and the soaked and drained porcini in the olive oil and add to the white sauce.
5 Stir in the Parma ham slivers. Add the cream and parsley, season, and bring to the boil. Turn off the heat.
6 To assemble the lasagne, butter a gratin dish and cover the bottom with a layer of pasta, then spread over a layer of sauce, dot with butter and sprinkle with some parmesan. Continue the process, making layer after layer, finishing with a layer of sauce and a sprinkling of parmesan. Cook in an oven preheated to 220°C/425°F/Gas Mark 7 for 20-25 minutes, or until bubbling and pale golden.
7 Serve with a little truffle oil splashed on top, and a little more parmesan.

FISH *fish*

MIXED FISH

& Shellfish Baked in Parchment with Summer Herbs & Vegetables

There is only one part of Italy which is more than 100 miles from the sea, which is why we have a great tradition of seafood dishes. Lots of recipes combine fish and shellfish in soups and stews. Some chefs make their own special sauces, they are secret actually, no one will tell how they make these sauces and just this one recipe can make a lot of difference with the flavours.

Serves four

1 8 scallops
2 500g/1 lb mussels
3 225g/8 oz salmon
4 225g/8 oz turbot
5 225g/8 oz halibut
6 sea salt and freshly ground black pepper
7 8 mangetout, topped and tailed
8 115g/4oz fine beans, topped and tailed
9 8 tiny new potatoes in their skins
10 225g/8 oz courgette, cut into slim lengths
11 fresh basil, chervil and chives, chopped
12 herb/garlic or extra virgin olive oil

To prepare

1 *Cut 4 x 14 inch diameter circles of baking parchment and butter one side. Scrub, debeard and dry the mussels, slice the scallops into 2 or 3 pieces, leaving the coral intact. Cut the fish into 1 inch cubes.*

2 *Blanch the beans in boiling salted water, leaving them crisp. Strain and refresh in cold water and drain.*

3 *Boil the potatoes until just cooked.*

4 *Divide all the fish and vegetables (cooked & raw) between the 4 circles of baking parchment, arranging them on one half of each paper circle, strew with the fresh herbs , grind over the salt and pepper and fold across the parchment, rolling the edges tightly. Staple the edges at one inch intervals.*

5 *Bake in a preheated oven 190ºC/375ºF/GM5 on a heavy baking sheet for about 15 mins. The bag will puff up and colour.*

6 *Serve immediately in a hot soup plate - tear the bags open and drizzle in a little oil.*

FISH

MONKFISH
Leek & White Bean Casserole

Serves six

1   3tblsp olive oil
2   2 leeks, white part only, thinly sliced
3   2cloves garlic, crushed
4   1.25 k-1.45k (2½-3lb) monkfish tail
5   250ml (8fl oz) dry white wine
6   1.1 litre (2pts) fish, chicken, or vegetable stock
7   1x400g tin cannellini beans, drained and rinsed

8   2 large tomatoes, peeled, deseeded and chopped
9   1tblsp flat-leaved parsley, chopped
10 1tblsp basil, chopped
11 salt and freshly ground black pepper
12 drops of fresh lemon juice
13 1bag trimmed young spinach

Garnish: Basil Aioli

To prepare

1   Place the wine in a saucepan and reduce to half, then add the stock and reduce again by about a quarter to intensify the flavours.
2   In a large saucepan, heat the olive oil and sauté the leeks and garlic until soft but not brown. Add the reduced wine and stock mixture. Simmer, covered, for approximately 3 minutes.
3   Meanwhile, prepare the monkfish by removing any brownish outer membranes. Cut off the 2 fillets and divide these into medallions

about 1cm thick. (The bone and trimmings can be used to make stock).
4   Now add the monkfish, beans, tomatoes, parsley, and basil. Bring to the boil, then simmer for 1 minute. Season to taste with salt and pepper and drops of the lemon juice.
5   To serve, place 3 or 4 spinach leaves in warm soup bowls. Ladle the hot casserole over the spinach. Garnish with a dollop of basil aioli.

Basil Aioli

1   2 egg yolks
2   2 cloves garlic, crushed
3   a generous handful of basil leaves

4   2 tblsp lemon juice
5   290ml (½pt) vegetable oil
6   salt and freshly ground white pepper

To prepare

1   In a food blender or processor, combine the egg yolks, garlic and basil.
2   Blend until well pureed. With the motor running, slowly add the oil to form an emulsion.

The mixture should be thick but not stiff.

3   Season with lemon juice, salt and pepper to taste.
4   Cover and store refrigerated for up to 1 week.

MUSSELS RISOTTO

Serves four

1 1kg/2lb potatoes
2 300g/10oz arborio rice
3 500g/1lb mussels
4 100g/3oz grated parmesan
5 handful of parsley, chopped

6 1 onion, chopped
7 4tblsp olive oil
8 170g/6oz peeled tomato, chopped
9 salt and freshly ground black pepper

'This is another speciality from Bari, just like saltimbocca is from Rome.'

To prepare

1 Pre-heat the oven to 180ºC/375ºF
Gas Mark 4
2 Clean the mussels
3 Peel the potatoes and slice.
4 Put a layer of potato in bottom of an oven proof casserole.
5 Scatter over the chopped onions, half the parsley, half the cheese and seasoning.

6 Add the mussels to the casserole and cover with rice.
7 Add tomato, the remaining onions, parsley, cheese, olive oil and seasoning.
8 Finish with the rest of the potato.
9 Add sufficient water to cover the top layer and put in oven for 60 mins

FISH

FRIED SEA BASS
Fillets with Saffron Mash & Salsa Verde

Salsa verde is a garlic-oil based sauce. Italians love it and it is used as an accompaniment to many dishes. It is strong and aromatic and peps up what would otherwise be a plain stew, soup or grill. Use the best oil from the first pressings of the olives. There are lots of myths about garlic, who knows which ones are true. What I do know is that garlic gives strength and keeps away colds and flu.

Serves four
1   750g (1½lb sea bass fillet, skin on, divided into 4 equal portions
2   2tblsp olive oil
3   25g/1oz butter

4   salt and freshly ground black pepper
5   1 quantity salsa verde

For the Saffron Mash
1   1.25kg (2½lbs) floury potatoes, such as Maris Piper or King Edward, peeled and cut into chunks
2   1 clove garlic, crushed
3   50ml/2 fl oz olive oil

4   a generous pinch of saffron soaked in 1tbsp hot water
5   a little milk or cream
6   freshly ground white pepper

'Salsa verde you can also use with meat, actually. Cook it plainly then put this green sauce on top.'

For the Salsa Verde
1   3 tblsp fresh flat-leaved parsley, roughly chopped
2   3tblsp basil, roughly chopped
3   1 tblsp fresh mint, roughly chopped
4   3 tblsp capers
5   6 anchovy fillets

6   1 clove garlic, chopped
7   1 tsp Dijon mustard
8   juice of half a lemon
9   100ml/4 fl oz extra virgin olive oil
10 1 tsp salt

To prepare
1   Begin by making the mash. Boil the potatoes for 15-20 minutes.
2   Drain, mash and beat in the garlic, olive oil, saffron infusion and a little milk to form a soft mash. Season with salt and freshly ground pepper. Keep warm.
3   Meanwhile make the salsa verde. Blend together all the ingredients for it in a food processor or a mortar and pestle to form a thick paste.
4   To cook the sea bass, melt the olive oil

and butter together in a large frying pan.
5   Season the sea bass with salt and pepper. Fry on both sides, taking care not to overcook. If cut from a small (450-900g/1-2 lbs) fish allow about two minutes on each side but up to 5 minutes on each side 1f the fillets are thick.
6   Serve the sea bass on a mould of mash, garnished with a spoonful of salsa verde

TUNA STEAK
with Fresh Herb Sauce

Serves four

1 4x5oz fresh tuna steaks

2 2 tblsp olive oil

For the sauce

1 150ml/5fl oz extra-virgin olive oil

2 50ml/2fl oz freshly squeezed lemon juice

3 ½ tsp coriander seeds, crushed coarsely

4 8 large basil leaves

5 2 plum tomatoes, blanched, deseeded and cut into small pieces

6 fresh chervil to garnish

To prepare

1 Season the tuna steaks. Heat 2tblsp olive oil in a medium sized frying pan. When very hot fry the fish for about 2 minutes on each side, depending on the thickness of the steaks. Do not allow to overcook. Keep warm.

2 To make the sauce: Heat the extra-virgin olive oil, lemon juice and coriander seeds in a small pan, bring to the boil, remove from the heat and add the basil leaves. Just before serving add the diced tomato and season well.

3 Serve the tuna sprinkled with the herb oil.

FISH

FILLET OF RED MULLET
with Fresh Herbs

Serves four
1 4 red mullet, each approx. 4oz, filleted or(4 trout)
2 1tblsp chopped fresh marjoram and basil
3 1tblsp white breadcrumbs
4 1tblsp olive oil
5 1 quantity of pesto sauce

'In Italy, herbs are king. Liguria is full of basil and marjoram, and this is one way of using them.'

To prepare
1 Clean the fillets. Set aside to dry on absorbent paper.
2 Mix the fresh herbs with the breadcrumbs and a little of the olive oil to make a smooth paste.
3 Re-shape the fish by taking two fillets and stuffing some of the paste mixture between them.
4 Preheat the oven to 190°C/375°F Gas Mark 5.
5 Put a little olive oil in a non-stick frying pan, and seal the fish parcels on both sides.
6 Place in the oven for 5minutes.
7 Serve the fish drizzled with pesto sauce.

STUFFED SQUID
in Tomato Sauce

Serves six
1 6 whole squid "tubes" about 11-13cm/4-5inches long

For the stuffing
1 1 egg
2 1 tblsp olive oil
3 1 clove garlic
4 3 tblsp parmesan cheese, freshly grated
5 4 tblsp fresh white breadcrumbs
6 125g/4oz peeled prawns, chopped
7 salt
8 one quantity of homemade tomato sauce or a bottle of tomato passata
9 4 tblsp olive oil

'Squid is one of my favourites, and this is a good recipe for it.'

To prepare
1 Mix together all the stuffing ingredients and use it to fill the cleaned squid tubes. Only two-thirds fill them because they will shrink as they cook.
2 Close the tops off with cocktail sticks.
3 Choose a shallow pan that will hold the squid in a single layer.
4 Add the olive oil and sauté the squid on all sides until browned.
5 Pour in the prepared tomato sauce, bring to a simmer and cook gently for 45-50 minutes or until tender.
6 Don't forget to remove the cocktail sticks before serving!!

MEAT
meat

CHICKEN FILLETS
with Parma Ham, Sage & Cheese

Saltimbocca is a well-loved traditional recipe of veal, Parma ham, sage and fontina. This is a variation on the theme using chicken breast.

Serves four

1 3 large chicken breasts
2 115g/4 oz Fontina cheese
3 115g/4 oz Parma ham
4 12 sage leaves
5 25g/1 oz butter
6 salt & freshly ground pepper

To prepare

1 Cut each chicken breast into four diagonal slices.
2 Flatten the slices by lightly beating them between damp sheets of clingfilm.
3 Slice the Fontina into 12 pieces.
4 Cut the Parma ham into pieces the same size as the flattened chicken slices. Now place on each chicken slice a piece of Fontina and season with salt and freshly ground black pepper and one sage leaf.
5 Cover with the Parma ham. In a large frying pan heat the butter until it foams, place the chicken pieces ham-side-down into the hot butter and fry briefly, then turn over.
6 Continue to cook until you see the Fontina melting and the chicken is cooked. Serve immediately.

'Chicken breasts are probably the most eaten food in the world! You can do them so many ways, and they are good athlete's food.'

MEAT

BEEF STEW
with Wild Mushrooms

Serves eight

1   2k/4½lb stewing steak, cut into large pieces
2   4 carrots, peeled and cut into rounds
3   3 medium onions, peeled and chopped
4   2 cloves garlic
5   1 sprig flat-leaved parsley
6   1 celery stalk, roughly chopped
7   3 bay leaves
8   1 tbsp fresh thyme or 1 tsp dried thyme
9   60ml/2½ fl oz brandy
10 1 bottle full-bodied red wine
11 60ml/2½fl oz plus 1 tbsp extra virgin olive oil
12 1 tsp whole black peppercorns
13 3 whole cloves
14 45g/11½oz butter
15 15g/½oz dried ceps, soaked in hot water for 20 mins
16 225g/½lb mixed fresh mushrooms, sliced
17 1 tbsp tomato puree
18 salt and freshly ground black pepper

To prepare

1   One day ahead, marinate the meat. In a non-reactive bowl combine the meat with the carrots, onions, garlic, parsley, celery, bay leaves, thyme, brandy, red wine and 1 tbsp olive oil. Tie the peppercorns and cloves in a piece of muslin and add to the marinade. Cover and keep in a cool place for 24 hours, stirring occasionally.

2   Remove the meat from the marinade, pat dry. Place the muslin bags in a flameproof casserole and strain the liquid from the marinade onto them. Add the soaking liquid from the ceps. Bring to the boil and simmer for 5 mins to reduce slightly. Remove from the heat.

3   Melt the butter with the remaining olive oil in a frying pan over a high heat.

4   Add the meat and brown. Do this in small batches if necessary.

5   Transfer to the casserole with the reduced marinade and the soaked dried ceps. In the same frying pan, saute the reserved vegetables until browned, transfer to the casserole.

6   Add the fresh mushrooms to the frying pan and saute until lightly browned. Set aside

7   Stir the tomato paste into the casserole, bring to a simmer and place in a preheated oven 180ºC/350ºF/Gas Mark 4 for 1½hrs until the meat is tender.

8   Season to taste, add the mushrooms, discard the muslin bag and bring back to simmering. Serve with potatoes, rice or pasta.

LAMB RAGU
With Rosemary

Serves four

1 1tsp tomato puree
2 1lge clove garlic, crushed
3 500g/1lb minced lamb
4 1lge onion, finely chopped
5 1 sprig fresh or large pinch of dried rosemary
6 200ml/7fl oz red wine
7 1 tin plum tomatoes,
8 salt and freshly ground black pepper
9 350g/12oz dried tagliatelle
10 parmesan or feta cheese shavings to serve
11 sprig of fresh rosemary to garnish

'Most of the time we eat ragu on a Sunday, when the whole family comes together. You make a big sauce that you can use with the pasta course too.'

To prepare

1 Brown the minced lamb in a heavy based pan on the boiling plate, stirring to break down any lumps.
2 Remove the mince and set aside.
3 Add the onions to the pan with the rosemary and fry together until the onion is soft and golden – about 10 minutes.
4 Lift the tomatoes from the tin, squeeze out and discard the juice and seeds, then liquidise the flesh with the tin juices
5 Return the mince to the pan, keep over a high heat and stir in the wine. It should bubble immediately. Scrape the bottom of the pan to loosen any crusty bits then leave the wine to bubble until reduced by half).
6 Stir in the liquidised tomatoes, tomato puree and garlic, season and cover. Simmer gently for about1 hour. Add water if it gets too thick.
7 Cook the tagliatelle in boiling salted water for about 10 minutes; drain.
8 Stir in the lamb ragu, sprinkle the cheese over, garnish with rosemary and serve.

DUCK
Alla Veronese

Serves four

1 4 x 5oz/4 x 150g duckling breasts
2 4oz/110g black grapes
3 2oz/50g onions
4 2floz/50ml port wine
5 8floz/225ml red grape juice
6 1/2 oz/15g cornflour
7 salt and pepper

To garnish

1 watercress
2 4 tomato roses

'I love the way Claudio from O' Sole Mio does the ducks that I shoot.'

To prepare

1 *Pre-heat the oven to 350ºF/180ºC/Gas Mark 4.*
2 *Trim fat and skin from Duck. Place Duck in an oven-proof dish.*
3 *Season Duck and add 4floz/110ml of water. Cover dish with aluminium foil.*
4 *Halve the grapes and remove the pips. Then cover the duck with grapes. Chop onions finely and sweat in the port until the liquid is reduced by half. Add the grape juice to the pan and simmer gently for 10 minutes.*
5 *Thicken the sauce with cornflour for another 5 minutes. Season sauce and pour over duck. Return the dish to the oven for 30 minutes. Basting frequently.*
6 *Remove the duck to a warmed serving platter and garnish.*

VEAL ESCALLOPES

Serves four

1. 500g/1lb veal escallopes
2. salt and freshly ground blackpepper
3. 750g/1½lbs peeled tomatoes, chopped
4. 2cloves garlic
5. 50g/2oz grated parmesan cheese
6. 4tblsp parsley,chopped
7. 150ml/5floz white wine
8. 4tblsp olive oil
9. cocktail sticks

To prepare

1. Mix together the garlic, parsley, parmesan cheese, salt and pepper.
2. Place a spoonful of mixture down the centre of each escallope.
3. Roll up and secure with a cocktail stick.
4. Fry the parcel in vegetable oil until browned on all sides. Drain and set aside.
5. In a large saucepan fry the onions in oil until they are golden
6. Add the white wine and stir in tomatoes and season.
7. Simmer the sauce uncovered for 15 minutes until thickened then add the veal parcels.
8. Simmer gently for a further 30 minutes.
9. Remove the cocktail sticks before serving.

MEAT

SLOW ROAST PORK
in Herbs & Wine

Serves four

1   1.35k/3lbs boned, rolled leg of pork, rind removed
2   1 clove garlic
3   8 sage leaves
4   salt & freshly ground black pepper
5   1 medium onion, chopped

6   1 leek, trimmed, washed & chopped
7   2 celery stalks, chopped
8   1 carrot, peeled & chopped
9   2 sprigs of fresh rosemary
10   half bottle dry white wine

For the sauce:

1   2 tbsp dry white wine
2   300ml / ½ pint double cream

3   salt and freshly ground black pepper

To prepare

1   Pre-heat the oven to 400ºF/200ºC/Gas Mark 6.
2   Peel the garlic and cut into slivers.
3   Using a pointed knife make several incisions into the pork leg and push into each a piece of sage and some garlic. Rub over with salt and pepper.
4   Line a small roasting tin with foil. Mix together the prepared vegetables and place in a layer in the lined tin.
5   Stand the pork joint on top and tuck the rosemary underneath it.
6   Add the wine. Leave the foil open and place the roasting tin in the middle of the oven for 20 minutes. Draw up the foil over the meat and lower the temperature to 325ºF/160ºC/Gas Mark

3 and continue cooking for 2 hours (or allow 35 mins /lb or 70 mins/kilo).
7   When the meat is cooked and tender, lift it out and rest on a carving board while you make the sauce.
8   Strain the juices from the roasting tin into a saucepan.
9   Squeeze the vegetables to extract all the flavour and discard them.
10   Add the wine to the juices, bring to the boil and reduce by a third, add the cream and boil again until the sauce is thickened.
11   Season and serve with the carved meat.
12   Grilled Mediterranean vegetables make a good accompaniment.

BAKED GUINEA FOWL
with Wild Mushrooms

Serves four

1 2 oven-ready Guinea fowl
2 25g/1oz butter, softened
3 5tblsp sherry vinegar
4 1 onion, roughly chopped
5 2 carrots, roughly chopped
6 2 celery sticks, roughly chopped
7 3 fresh bay leaves
8 15g/½oz dried porcini mushrooms
9 4tblsp mushroom ketchup
10 300ml/½ pt red wine, or wine and port mixed
11 500ml/1pt fresh chicken or game stock
12 salt and freshly ground black pepper

For the kneaded butter

1 50g/2oz butter, softened
2 25g/1 oz plain flour

To finish

1 170g/6oz wild or flat black mushrooms, sliced
2 Sprigs of fresh thyme to garnish

To prepare

1 Smear the guinea fowl all over with the softened butter. Lay on their sides in a large roasting tin and roast for 20 minutes at 230°C/450°F/Gas Mark 8.

2 Turn the birds over and roast for a further 20 minutes. Remove from the oven - they should be quite rare.

3 Cool a little, then remove the legs and cut the breast off the bone. Place the legs under a preheated grill and cook for 4-5 minutes on each side. Arrange the legs in the bottom of a large, shallow ovenproof dish and place the breast meat on top.

4 Break up the carcasses and place in a large saucepan. Add the sherry vinegar to the roasting tin, scraping to dislodge any sediment, then add to the carcass stock pot with the remaining ingredients.

5 Slowly bring to the boil, turn down the heat and simmer for 1 hour. Strain the stock into a jug and return to the pan.

6 Bring to a fast boil and reduce to 500ml/ 1 pint. Season.

7 Make the kneaded butter by mixing the butter and flour to a smooth paste. Gradually whisk the kneaded butter into the stock, bring to the boil and bubble until syrupy. Add the mushrooms to the sauce.

8 Pour over the game and cover. Place in the oven at 180°C/350°F/Gas Mark 4, and cook for about 45 minutes, or until hot to the centre. Garnish with sprigs of thyme.

MEAT

DESSERTS

desserts

RHUBARB
Strawberry & Orange Compote

Serves six

1 6 small oranges

2 500g/1 lb young pink rhubarb, trimmed weight

3 90g-115g/3-4 oz caster sugar

4 225g/8 oz strawberries

To prepare

1 Remove the zest of 2 oranges and cut into thin strips.

2 Cut the rhubarb into 1 inch lengths.

3 Dissolve 90g/3 oz of sugar in 1 pint water over a low heat.

4 Bring to the boil and toss in the orange zest and boil for 2-3 mins. Remove the zest and set aside.

5 Add the rhubarb to the pan and bring back to the boil. Place a lid on the pan and remove from the heat. The rhubarb will continue to cook in the hot syrup without losing it's shape.

6 Meanwhile, remove all the peel and pith from the oranges and slice into rounds. When the rhubarb has cooled, transfer it to a serving dish with a slotted spoon, taste the syrup for sweetness and add the remaining sugar, if liked.

7 Heat the syrup to dissolve the extra sugar, and boil over a fierce heat until reduced and sticky.

8 Add the reserved orange zest, cook for a further minute, cool a little and pour over the rhubarb. Stir in the orange segments. Cool, cover and chill.

9 Just before serving, hull the strawberries and either halve or quarter, and stir into the compote. Serve chilled.

DESSERTS

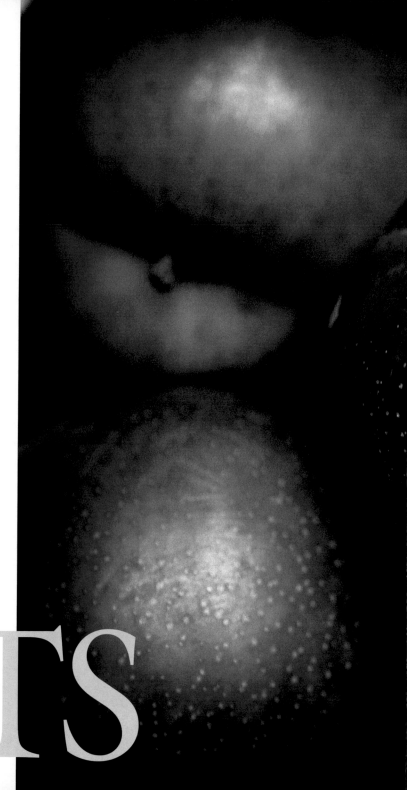

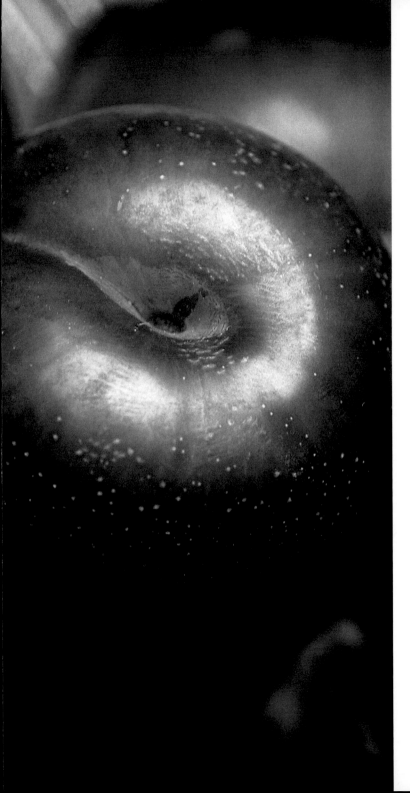

PLUMS
on Panetone with Marzipan

Serves six

1 125g/4oz unsalted butter, softened
2 6 slices panettone, about ½ inch thick
(day-old bread is best)
3 500g/1 lb ripe plums

4 125g/4oz caster sugar
5 140g/5oz marzipan (ready-made)
6 90g/3oz slivered almonds
7 3 tblsp Cointreau

To serve

Creme fraiche

To prepare

1 Preheat the oven to 180°C/350°F/Gas Mark 4.

2 Use almost all the butter to cover the panetone on both sides. Place the slices on a baking sheet.

3 Halve and stone the plums and arrange as many halves as will fit on to each slice of bread, cut side uppermost, then dredge with half the sugar.

4 Place a knob of marzipan in each plum cavity and scatter over the almonds and Cointreau.

5 Sprinkle with a little more sugar and dot with the remaining butter. Cover with a piece of buttered greaseproof paper. Bake for 40-45 minutes, uncovering and sprinkling with the remaining sugar halfway through cooking. The panetone should be crisp and golden and the marzipan browned. Serve warm with creme fraiche.

TIRAMISU

Serves four

1. 3 eggs
2. 150g/5oz caster sugar
3. 250g/8oz mascarpone cheese
4. strong black coffee
5. cocoa powder for sprinkling
6. one packet sariardi biscuits or boudoir biscuits
7. pinch of salt

To prepare

1. Separate the eggs.
2. Whisk egg white with a pinch of salt.
3. Gradually whisk in sugar.
4. Whisk mascarpone into mixture a little at a time.
5. Pour some into a shallow wide glass dish.
6. Dip biscuits in coffee and make a single layer on top of the mascarpone mixture.
7. Sprinkle cocoa powder over surface.
8. Repeat the layers to fill the dish ending with a layer of mascarpone.
9. Sprinkle with cocoa powder
10. Chill and serve.

BAKED AMARETTO
Pudding

Serves six-eight

1. 75g(3oz) amaretto biscuits
2. 350ml(12fl oz) whole milk
3. 300ml(10fl oz) single cream
4. 5 large eggs
5. 75g(3oz) caster sugar
6. 2tblsp Amaretto
7. 2tblsp Marsala
8. 75g(3oz) plain chocolate, finely chopped

For the caramel

1. 75g(3oz) caster sugar

To prepare

1. Start by making the caramel. Put the caster sugar and 2tblsp of water in a small heavy-based saucepan, stir over a medium heat, and then bring to the boil. Boil rapidly without stirring. When the syrup begins to turn golden brown, withdraw the pan quickly from the heat and pour the syrup into a soufflé dish. Tip the dish in all directions to coat the sides and bottom evenly, then set aside while you make the pudding.
2. Pour the milk and cream into another pan and bring to simmering point. Meanwhile, in a large bowl, beat the eggs and sugar until combined, then add the amaretto and Marsala.
3. Remove the milk and cream from the heat and add the chocolate, then stir until melted and thoroughly combined.
4. Finally, pour this mixture over the egg mixture in a slow stream, beating constantly.
5. Crush the amaretto biscuits until reduced to the texture of fine breadcrumbs, and then mix into the egg and milk mixture. Leave to one side for 15 minutes.
6. Preheat the oven to 150ºC/300ºF Gas Mark 2. Now pour the mixture into the soufflé dish and place the whole thing in a roasting tin. Add enough boiling water to more or less fill the roasting tin.
7. Place the tin on the bottom shelf of the oven. Cook for about 1 hour, until set. To test if it is ready, insert the thin blade of a knife or skewer into the middle of the pudding – it should come out clean.
8. Remove from the roasting tin and set aside to cool to room temperature. Once cooled, chill in the fridge for at least 4 hours.
9. To unmould, loosen it all round with a palette knife. Then, place a round plate over the soufflé dish and turn the dish over on to the plate. Give a few sharp jerks to the soufflé dish, then lift it away – it should come away clean.

DESSERTS

107

ALMOND PANNACOTTA
with Orange & Lemon Grappa Sauce

Serves eight

1 2 tblsp powdered gelatine or 4 leaves of sheet gelatine
2 4 tblsp warm water (only if you are using powdered gelatine)
3 570ml/1pt full milk
4 6 tblsp sugar
5 6 large egg yolks
6 1tsp vanilla extract
7 450ml/1pt whipping cream
8 2-4 tblsp Amaretto liqueur
9 oil for the moulds
10 8 x 150ml/5fl oz dariole moulds or ramekins

To prepare

1 Sprinkle the powdered gelatine over the warm water, or soak the leaves of gelatine in cold water.
2 Bring the milk to the boil, whisk the egg yolks and sugar lightly and stir in the hot milk.
3 Return the mixture to a clean pan and cook over a low heat stirring constantly until the custard is smooth and thickened. It is ready when it coats the back of the wooden spoon.
4 Remove the pan from the heat and add the vanilla extract and Amaretto liqueur stirring well.
5 Whisk in the softened gelatine and continue to stir until it has completely dissolved.
6 Strain the mixture into a bowl and place the bowl in a larger one containing ice cubes. Leave the mixture until it becomes syrupy (like unbeaten egg white in consistency), stirring from time to time.
7 Whip the cream to soft peaks. Lightly whisk in the Amaretto liqueur. Fold the cream into the custard mixture.
8 Lightly oil the moulds and fill with the mixture.
9 Chill for at least 8 hours, or overnight.
10 Half an hour before serving, turn out the mixture by dipping the moulds very briefly in hot water. Hold a wetted serving plate over each mould, turn the two over together and shake the mould once or twice before removing.
11 Serve with orange and lemon grappa sauce.

Orange & Lemon Grappa Sauce

1 500g/1lb caster sugar
2 300ml/½pt hot water, mixed with the juice and finely grated
zest of 1 orange and 1 lemon
3 1 lemon, scrubbed
4 2tblsp lemon grappa

To prepare

1 Dissolve the sugar in one pint water over a gentle heat, stirring all the time. Turn up the heat, let the syrup bubble until it turns pale golden, then amber.
2 Off the heat, carefully pour in the hot citrus water and return the pan to a low heat. Stir the syrup with a wooden spoon until it is smooth and boiling gently.
3 Place the whole lemon in a container that has a lid; pour the syrup over and stir in the grappa.
4 When the sauce is cold, seal with the lid and leave for a few days to allow the flavours to develop.

DESSERTS

LIME & RASPBERRY
Tart

Serves six-eight: For the pastry
1 140g/5oz unsalted soft butter
2 1 large egg
3 30g/2oz caster sugar
4 pinch of salt
5 225g/8oz plain flour, plus a little extra

For the filling
1 4 eggs
2 115g/4oz caster sugar
3 finely grated zest and juice of 4 limes
4 1pt double cream
5 250g/8oz raspberries
6 icing sugar to dust

'If I am going to have a pudding, I prefer it to be a fruit tart to something very creamy.'

To prepare

1 To make the pastry: Cream the butter with the sugar, beat in the egg and the salt. Continue to beat until the mixture is light and fluffy. Then add in the flour and mix well. Tip onto a floured board and knead lightly into a ball, flatten slightly and wrap in cling film. Allow to rest somewhere cool for 30 minutes.

2 Preheat the oven to 190°C/375°F/Gas Mark 5.

3 Roll out the pastry to line a 9ins flan tin with removable base. Bake blind for 10 minutes. Remove the blind and return to the oven for a further 5 minutes. Remove from the oven and allow to cool a little.

4 Turn down the heat to 180°C/350°F/Gas Mark 4. Meanwhile, make the filling. Beat together the eggs and sugar until thoroughly blended, but not frothy. Beat in the lime zest and juice, then beat in the double cream.

5 Place the flan tin on a baking tray and arrange the raspberries on the pastry base. Carefully pour the lime custard into the pastry case and return the tart to the oven.

6 Cook for 30-35 minutes until the custard is just set in the centre. Serve warm or cold, dusted with icing sugar.

DESSERTS

DESSERTS

PASSION FRUIT
& Blood Orange Semi-Freddo

Serves eight

1   3 large egg whites
2   good pinch salt
3   225g/8 oz caster sugar
4   1 tbspn liquid glucose

5   150ml/half pint blood orange juice
6   4-5 passion fruit
7   juice of one large lemon
8   300ml/½ pint whipping cream

To prepare

1   Whisk the egg whites and the salt until they stand in soft peaks.

2   Mix together the orange and lemon juices and pour into a saucepan.

3   Cut the passion fruits in half and scoop out the flesh into the citrus juices.

4   Add the sugar and glucose and dissolve over a low heat. Bring to the boil then briefly liquidise and strain the juices to remove the passion fruit pips.

5   Return to the heat and boil fiercely for about three minutes.

6   Pour immediately in a thin stream onto the egg whites whisking all the time at high speed.

7   Continue whisking until the mixture looks like uncooked meringue. Cool.

8   Whisk the cream in a separate bowl until thick but not stiff and gently fold into the meringue-like mixture. Transfer to a suitable container and freeze for at least 3 hours. It should be soft enough to serve straight from the freezer.

SAUCES
Sauces

WALNUT
Pesto

1   large bunch flat-leaved parsley
2   90g/3 oz shelled walnuts
3   2 tbsp walnut oil
4   4-5 tbsp extra virgin olive oil
5   lemon juice

To prepare
1   Blitz the garlic, parsley and walnuts in a food processor, continue to whiz whilst adding the walnut oil and 3 tbsp of the olive oil in a steady stream.
2   Season well with salt and freshly ground black pepper and lemon juice.

FISH
Stock

Uses: soups, sauces, stews & poaching
1   1k(2lb) white fish bones & trimmings
2   1 onion, chopped
3   1 stick celery, chopped
4   1 carrot, chopped
5   ½ leek, chopped
6   4 parsley stalks
7   1 sprig thyme
8   1 bay leaf
9   1 tsp black peppercorns
10 2 tblsp vegetable oil

To prepare
1   Thoroughly rinse the fish bones and trimmings under cold water. Drain and set aside.
2   In a large saucepan combine the oil and vegetables over a low heat. Cook until softened (about 5 mins).
3   Add the fish bones and trimmings and cook for a further 5 mins.
4   Add all remaining ingredients and cover with cold
water. Bring to the boil, skimming off any scum that rises to the surface.
5   Cover and simmer very gently for 30 mins. Strain through a very fine sieve and leave to cool.

CHICKEN
Stock

Makes approx 3-4litres/6 pts
1   3-4litres/6pts water
2   1.5kg/3lb raw chicken carcass or bony joints
3   2 carrots, chopped
4   1 stick celery, chopped
5   2 whole leeks, chopped
6   1 onions, chopped
7   bay leaf, sprig thyme
8   1 tsp black peppercorns

To prepare
1   Place the chicken carcass or bones, vegetables and seasonings in a deep saucepan and add the cold water.
2   Bring the water to the boil and then skim off any scum that comes to the surface.
3   Boil for 5 minutes then turn down the heat and simmer for a minimum of 2 hours, but preferably 3-4 hours.
4   Pass through a sieve, then through wet muslin. Keep in a covered bowl in the refrigerator for up to 3 days, or freeze.

Dark Chicken Stock

First roast the carcass in an oven pre-heated to 200ºC/400ºF/GM6 for about 20 minutes, turning frequently. Drain off the fat and proceed as above.

SAUCES

BASIC TOMATO
Sauce for Pasta

Serves four
1 1x400g/14oz tin peeled plum tomatoes
2 1 small onion, peeled and very finely chopped
3 2 tblsp virgin olive oil
4 1 small clove garlic, peeled and crushed
5 1 small dried chilli, crumbled
6 1 tsp sugar
7 salt and freshly ground black pepper

To prepare
1 Lift the tomatoes out of the tin, split them open and squeeze out and discard the watery liquid in the middle of each. Place in a food processor, along with the juices from the tin, and blend to a puree
2 In a medium pan, soften the onion in the oil over a medium heat for about 10 minutes, until soft. Add a little water as the onions cook to prevent browning.
3 When the onion is soft, add the sugar, garlic, chilli, and tomato, and then bring to the boil and cook over a lively heat for no more than three minutes.
4 Taste and adjust the seasoning, then remove from the heat and allow to cool. Store in the refrigerator.

PESTO
Sauce

1 1 clove garlic, finely chopped
2 2fl oz olive oil
3 25g/1oz finely chopped basil
4 2oz pine kernels
5 25g/1 oz freshly grated parmesan cheese

To prepare
1 Place the basil, garlic, pine nuts and parmesan cheese in a food processor, whiz until smooth.
2 Continue processing and drizzle in the olive oil.
3 To store the pesto place in small sterilized jars and float some olive oil on the surface to seal. Keep in a cool place for up to a week.

RED PESTO
Sauce

1 30g/1 oz fresh basil leaves
2 30g/1 oz freshly grated Parmesan cheese
3 ½oz pine nuts
4 50ml/2 fl oz olive oil
5 60g/2 oz sun dried tomatoes in oil
6 1 clove garlic (small)

To prepare
1 Place the basil, garlic, pine nuts and drained sun dried tomatoes in a food processor, whiz until smooth.
2 Continue processing and drizzle in the olive oil. Stir in the parmesan cheese.
3 To store the pesto place in small sterilized jars and float some olive oil on the surface to seal. Keep in a cool place for up to a week.

SAUCES

ACKNOWLEDGEMENTS

Many people combined to make this book possible. Special thanks are due to
Lorenzo Amoruso himself for sharing his cooking tips and recipes; his mamma for
inspiring and giving him a love of food; Tony Cimmino and Claudio Nardoni,
owners of O' Sole Mio Restaurant in Glasgow, for the use of their premises in our
photo shoot; photographer Alan Peebles; Vital editor Kay Cox and designer
Lesley Redfern. Thanks also to Mo Scott for her very helpful advice and guidance.